This book belongs to

Delectables
For All Seasons

Maryjo Koch

Coffee

SWANS ISLAND BOOKS

CollinsPublishersSanFrancisco

A Division of HarperCollinsPublishers

PUBLISHED IN 1995 BY
COLLINS PUBLISHERS SAN FRANCISCO
1160 BATTERY STREET
SAN FRANCISCO CA 94111

SWANS ISLAND BOOKS

LIBRARY OF CONGRESS CATALOGING-IN-PUBLICATION DATA

KOCH, MARYJO.
    COFFEE: DELECTABLES FOR ALL SEASONS / MARYJO KOCH.
        P.   CM.
    "SWANS ISLAND BOOKS."
    ISBN 0-00-255479-8
    1. COFFEE.
TX817.C6K63   1995
641.6'373 — DC20   94-31807
                                           CIP

PRINTED IN HONG KONG
10 9 8 7 6 5 4 3 2 1

Greetings from The Land of Coffee

COFFEE

"COFFEE MY ONE ONLY BLISS IS,
SWEETER THAN THOUSANDS OF KISSES,
BETTER THAN SPARKLING WINE."

THE CANTATA NO. 211 (THE COFFEE CANTATA)
JOHANN SEBASTIAN BACH, 1732

The Divine Shrub

The coffee plant, a member of the madder family, is an evergreen shrub with petite white blossoms, whose scent is reminiscent of gardenias. The blooms' heady nectar is ambrosia for insects, who often feast gratis because arabica coffee plants are self-fertilizing.

Coffee plants flourish only in countries lying between the Tropics of Cancer and Capricorn—the lands of eternal summer.

The continuous cycle by which the coffee plant bears its red cherry-like fruit depends on rainfall. If it rains ten times in one year, the plant will flower ten times, producing ripe fruit within six to eleven weeks depending on the species.

The explosive flowering transforms verdant mountains into fairylands of blossom snowflakes which billow into snow-like perfumed drifts in the wind.

The two most important species of coffee cultivated globally are arabica and robusta.

Coffee plantations grow their plants from either seeds or cuttings, preferably on shady slopes with an average temperature of 70 degrees F.

*T*HE BEST WAY TO HARVEST THE BERRIES INVOLVES A PAINSTAKING PROCESS TO INSURE THE HIGHEST QUALITY RESULT. THE RIPE RUBY BERRIES, OR DRUPES, ARE HANDPICKED ONE BY ONE. AFTER THE HARVEST, THE BERRIES ARE PROCESSED BY ONE OF TWO METHODS. SIXTY-FIVE PERCENT OF THE WORLD'S COFFEE IS STILL PREPARED BY THE TRADITIONAL DRY METHOD, RATHER THAN THE MODERN INDUSTRIAL WET METHOD.

THE DRY METHOD FIRST CALLS FOR WASHING THE COFFEE BERRIES, AFTER WHICH THEY ARE DRAINED AND SPREAD IN THIN LAYERS ON A CLOTH ON THE GROUND. WHILE THE FRUIT FERMENTS IT IS TURNED SEVERAL TIMES A DAY WITH A RAKE, THEN HEAPED AND COVERED AT NIGHT TO PREVENT EXPOSURE TO MOISTURE.

PROCESSING COFFEE FRUIT BY THE WET METHOD REQUIRES AN ABUNDANT WATER SUPPLY. THE FRUIT IS FERMENTED FOR TWELVE TO TWENTY- FOUR HOURS AFTER THE INITIAL WASHING BY MECHANICALLY REMOVING THE FLESHY OUTER PULP, THEN PLACING THE REMAINS IN LARGE CONCRETE SLUICEWAYS OR WASHING TANKS AND CONSTANTLY CHANGING THE WATER. AFTER WASHING, THE FRUIT IS SPREAD OUT ON THE GROUND TO DRAIN AND DRY AS IN THE DRY METHOD.

*A*FTER TWO OR THREE WEEKS, WHEN THOROUGHLY DRY, THE DRUPES ARE MILLED TO REMOVE THE HUSK KNOWN AS THE PARCHMENT AND THE THIN INNER SKIN KNOWN AS THE SILVER.

THE RESULT? THE NOBLE BEAN.

The Tale of the Tree

In 1714, the Burgomaster of Amsterdam presented to Louis XIV a robust five-foot-tall coffee tree from one of the Dutch colonial plantations in Java. Recognizing the tree's value, the Sun King ordered the construction of what was to be the first greenhouse built in France. The Royal Botanist tended the rare specimen carefully in the Jardin des Plants. In time, seedlings from "the tree" thrived.

Gabriel Mathieu de Clieu, Captain of the French Infantry on Martinique, made many vain attempts to obtain coffee seeds or seedlings from the Royal Botanist. He then appealed to the Royal Physician with assistance from a lady of quality, but got no further. Finally, by stealth one night, he succeeded in removing one small plant from the Jardin des Plants.

Café

25.

Seedling in hand, the captain set sail for the west indies. On the voyage, the tree's survival was threatened by jealousy, sabotage, pirates, storms and water rationing — but de clieu held all of these at bay. He was determined to be of service to his country by successfully cultivating coffee in the colonies.

Almost chocolate

Abundant early harvests permitted de clieu to extend significantly the cultivation of coffee on martinique, but it was a devastating hurricane two years later that cleared the way for coffee by decimating the island's main resource: cocoa trees.

By 1777 there were more than nineteen million coffee trees in martinique alone. Today, plantations in central and south america provide seventy-five percent of the world with coffee.

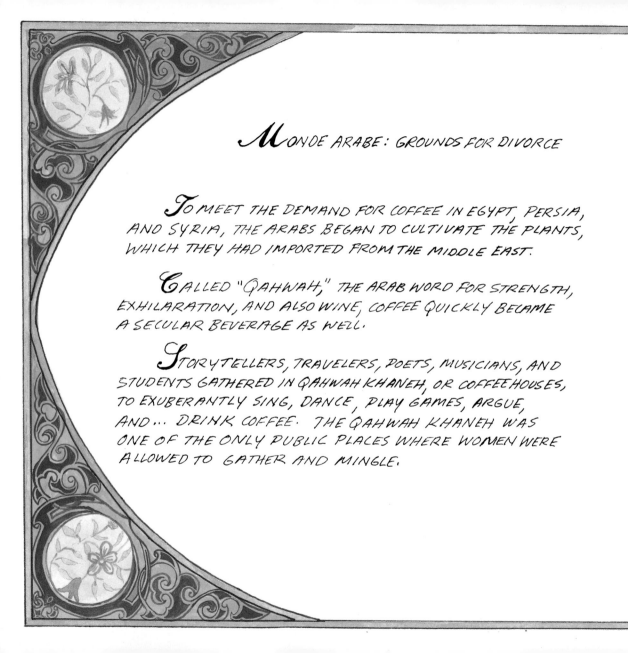

*M*onde Arabe: Grounds for Divorce

*T*o meet the demand for coffee in Egypt, Persia, and Syria, the Arabs began to cultivate the plants, which they had imported from the Middle East.

*C*alled "Qahwah," the Arab word for strength, exhilaration, and also wine, coffee quickly became a secular beverage as well.

*S*torytellers, travelers, poets, musicians, and students gathered in Qahwah Khaneh, or coffeehouses, to exuberantly sing, dance, play games, argue, and... drink coffee. The Qahwah Khaneh was one of the only public places where women were allowed to gather and mingle.

*A*TTEMPTS BY RELIGIOUS ZEALOTS TO CLOSE DOWN THE COFFEE HOUSES WERE THWARTED. RULERS SUSPICIOUS OF SUBVERSIVE INTELLECTUAL ACTIVITY WERE SEDUCED BY THE TAX REVENUE THE COFFEEHOUSES BROUGHT IN. WIVES CONCERNED ABOUT THEIR HUSBANDS' DEFECTION TO THE COFFEEHOUSE SOON SUCCUMBED TO THE BLACK BEVERAGE'S WILES. IN THE MARRIAGE CEREMONY, HUSBANDS PROMISED TO PROVIDE THEIR WIVES WITH COFFEE THROUGHOUT THEIR LIVES; FAILURE TO DO SO BECAME GROUNDS FOR DIVORCE.

KALDI AND THE GOATS

LEGENDS LINK COFFEE WITH PRIESTS, POETS, DOCTORS, AND PHILOSOPHERS. FROM ITS FIRST DISCOVERY AS A DRINK, COFFEE HAS BEEN SHROUDED IN MYSTERY, IMBUED WITH MAGICAL PROPERTIES, AND SURROUNDED WITH CONTROVERSY. THE FIRST COFFEE DRINKERS EXPERIENCED SENSATIONS RANGING FROM EXHILARATION TO RELIGIOUS ECSTASY.

*L*IKE ONE OF SCHEHERAZADE'S TALES FROM THE ARABIAN NIGHTS, THE TALE OF THE DARK BREW UNFOLDS IN AFRICA AT DAWN. A PASSING MUSLIM IMAM, WEARY FROM THE EFFORT TO REMAIN AWAKE DURING HIS NIGHTLY DEVOTIONS, STUMBLES UPON YOUNG KALDI THE GOATHERD. KALDI AND HIS GOATS GAMBOL AND PRANCE ABOUT IN A CLEARING BORDERED BY EVERGREEN SHRUBS WITH BRILLIANT SCARLET BERRIES. AFTER LEARNING THAT KALDI AND THE GOATS HAD EATEN THE FRUIT, THE MONK RETURNS TO THE MONASTERY AND SHARES HIS DISCOVERY WITH THE BRETHREN. THE MONKS REFINE THE STIMULANT BY DRYING AND BOILING THE BEANS.

*T*HE DEVOTED CARRY NEWS OF THE CELESTIAL DRAUGHT TO THE REST OF THE ISLAMIC WORLD DURING THEIR RELIGIOUS PILGRIMAGES.

Austria and Germany: Kipfel and Kaffeeklatsch

In 1683, Muhammad IV of Turkey marched 300,000 men off to conquer Europe. He laid siege to Vienna, but his strategy and secrets were revealed to the city's leaders by Franz George Kolschitzky, a Polish spy in their employ. Disguised as a Turk, the patron saint of Viennese coffee swam across the Danube to the Turkish encampments, where he gathered information between cups of coffee.

When the Turks fled, Kolschitzky claimed the sacks of beans they left behind and asked Austrians to reward him for his services by opening a store from which he might sell his coffee. Upon its opening his cafe, the Blue Bottle, served Kipfel, a pastry triumphantly baked in the shape of a crescent, the Muslim symbol that appears on the Turkish flag.

THOUGH THE GERMANS WERE SPARED A SHOWDOWN WITH THE TURKS, FREDRICH II, THE GREAT KING OF PRUSSIA (1740-86) FOUND AN ADVERSARY IN COFFEE. ANNOYED THAT SO MUCH MONEY WAS BLEEDING OUT OF HIS EMPIRE INTO FOREIGN COFFERS, HE MOUNTED A CAMPAIGN AGAINST THE BREW, AIDED BY PHYSICIANS WILLING TO DENOUNCE IT. IN RESPONSE, JOHANN SEBASTIAN BACH WROTE THE GOSSIPY "COFFEE CANTATA," WHICH POKED FUN AT THE KING'S BOMBASTIC CLAIMS ABOUT BEER. FREDRICH II PROCLAIMED THAT HE HAD GROWN UP ON THE SAME BEER THAT HAD NOURISHED GERMAN SOLDIERS FOR CENTURIES, AND THEREFORE RESPONSIBLE CITIZENS WERE TO DRINK BEER INSTEAD OF COFFEE. A SMALL ARMY OF COFFEE SPIES INFILTRATED THE CITIES, BUT THEY WERE DEFEATED BY THE INDOMITABLE HAUSFRAU, THE GERMAN HOUSEWIFE, WHO DELIGHTED IN SERVING THE DRINK TO FRIENDS. UNEASY HUSBANDS COINED THE TERM "KAFFEEKLATSCH" (COFFEE-GOSSIP), WHICH TODAY HAS COME TO MEAN A GET-TOGETHER.

COFFEE THROUGH THE AGES

 COFFEE ARABICA PLANTS GROW IN THE WILD IN KEFA (KAFFA), SOUTHWEST ETHIOPIA.

AFRICAN TRIBES CRUSHED RIPE COFFEE BERRIES, MIXED THEM WITH ANIMAL FAT, AND SHAPED THEM INTO BALLS FOR CONSUMPTION BY WAR PARTIES.

 850 A.D. A MUSLIM IMAM OBSERVES COFFEE BERRY-INTOXICATED GOATHERD CAVORTING WITH HIS GOATS AND RETURNS TO HIS MONASTERY WITH SOME BEANS. THE FRUIT PERMITS THE MONKS TO PRAY ALL NIGHT. THE ANGEL GABRIEL APPEARS TO MUHAMMAD IN A DREAM REVEALING THE NATURE OF THE BERRY.

1285 THE STARVING HEALER, DERVISH OMAR, SAMPLES THE BERRIES AND BOILS THEM, CREATING THE FIRST COFFEE BEVERAGE. COFFEE BEANS ARE FIRST ROASTED.

1454 PRESCRIBED AS A MEDICINE IN PERSIA BY SHEIKH GEMALEDDIN OF ADEN, COFFEE PLANTS ARE IMPORTED AND CULTIVATED IN ARABIA.

1511 COFFEE HOUSES OPEN IN CONSTANTINOPLE, MECCA, AND MEDINA; RELIGIOUS ZEALOTS ATTEMPT TO CLOSE THEM.

1615 VENETIANS IMPORT COFFEE INTO EUROPE FOR THE FIRST TIME.

1658 MUSLIM PILGRIMS SMUGGLE COFFEE SEEDS TO CEYLON, ENDING THE ARAB COFFEE MONOPOLY.

1658 THE FIRST COFFEE HOUSE OPENS IN LONDON.

1669 SULEIMAN AGA, TURKISH AMBASSADOR TO FRENCH KING LOUIS XIV, BRINGS COFFEE TO THE PARIS COURT AT HIS ELABORATE BASHES.

1670 DOROTHY JONES OPENS ONE OF THE FIRST COFFEE HOUSES IN AMERICA.

 1683 AUSTRIANS DEFEAT TURKS IN VIENNA, BUT COFFEE CONQUERS BEER AS THE POPULATION'S PALATE DISPLACES TRADITIONAL ALES WITH TURKISH COFFEE.

1689	CAFE DE PROCOPE OPENS IN PARIS.
1698	THE DUTCH BEGIN COFFEE CULTIVATION IN JAVA.
1720	CAFFE FLORIAN OPENS ON PIAZZA SAN MARCO, VENICE. IT REMAINS OPEN TODAY.
1714	THE BURGOMASTER OF AMSTERDAM SENDS A GIFT TO LOUIS XIV: A COFFEE PLANT TO BECOME KNOWN AS "THE TREE."
1723	FRENCH INFANTRY CAPTAIN GABRIEL DE CLIEU ILLICITLY PROCURES A SEEDLING FROM "THE TREE" FROM THE ROYAL JARDIN DE PLANTS AND TRANSPLANTS IT TO MARTINIQUE. IT LIVES TO BECOME THE PROGENITOR OF ALL COFFEE PLANTS CULTIVATED IN THE AMERICAS.
1773	KING GEORGE OF ENGLAND IMPOSES THE TEA TAX, PROMPTING AMERICAN COLONISTS TO ATTACK ENGLISH SHIPS IN BOSTON HARBOR. THE BOSTON TEA PARTY FORESHADOWS THE AMERICAN REVOLUTION: COFFEE IS ESTABLISHED AS THE NATIONAL BEVERAGE.
1783	BACH WRITES THE COFFEE CANTATA.
1822	ESPRESSO MACHINES APPEAR IN FRANCE.
1827	THE COFFEE PERCOLATOR IS INVENTED BY FRENCH JEWELER JACQUES AUGUSTIN GANDAIS.
1856	GAIL BORDEN, INVENTOR OF EVAPORATED MILK, RECEIVES BRITISH PATENT FOR A SOLUBLE COFFEE PREPARATION: INSTANT COFFEE.
1903	UNITED STATES GRANTS A PATENT TO A JAPANESE CHEMIST, DR. SATORI KATO, FOR PERFECTING INSTANT COFFEE CONCENTRATES.
1945	ACHILLE GAGGIA CREATES THE PISTON-POWERED ESPRESSO MACHINE.
1993	CAPPUCCINO IS CONSIDERED BY MANY BABY BOOMERS AS THE NEW AGE ANSWER FOR MOMENTARILY DRIVING AWAY THE BLUES.

" THERE WAS A TINY
RANGE WITHIN WHICH COFFEE WAS
EFFECTIVE, SHORT OF WHICH IT WAS USELESS,
AND BEYOND WHICH, IT WAS FATAL."

THE WRITING LIFE ANNIE DILLARD, 1989

"NEVER DRINK BLACK COFFEE AT LUNCH;
IT WILL KEEP YOU AWAKE IN THE AFTERNOON."

HOW TO SURVIVE FROM NINE TO FIVE   JILLY COOPER, 1970

" DRINKING LOTS OF COFFEE JUST
MAKES YOU A WIDE-AWAKE DRUNK."

ATTRIBUTED TO EDITOR AND FRIEND,

MAURA CAREY DAMACION,
1994

THE CURE

A PERSIAN SAGA REPORTS THAT
THE ARCHANGEL GABRIEL DELIVERED TO
THE PROPHET MUHAMMAD HIS FIRST CUP OF COFFEE.
THE PROPHET AFTERWARD DECLARED THAT HE FELT
"ABLE TO UNSEAT FORTY HORSEMEN AND POSSESS FIFTY
WOMEN."

SEVENTEENTH-CENTURY MEDICAL WISDOM RESPECTED
COFFEE AS "A WHOLSOM AND PHYSICAL DRINK, CLOSES THE ORAFICE
OF THE STOMACH, FORTIFIES HEAT WITHIN, HELPETH DIGESTION,
QUICKENETH THE SPIRITS, MAKETH THE HEART LIGHTSOME,
IS GOOD AGAINST EYESORES, COUGHS, COLDS, RHUMES,
CONSUMPTION, HEAD-ACH, DROPSIE, GOUT, SCURVY,
KINGS EVIL, AND MANY OTHERS."

ALL ABOUT COFFEE
WILLIAM UKERS, 1935

Buche De Noel

4 EGGS
½ TEASPOON SALT
¾ CUP SUGAR
2 TABLESPOONS UNSWEETENED COCOA
1 TEASPOON VANILLA
¾ CUP READY-MADE PANCAKE MIX
CONFECTIONERS' SUGAR
1 CUP WHIPPING CREAM
½ CUP FINE GRANULATED SUGAR
MOCHA-BUTTER CREAM FROSTING (BELOW)

GREASE BOTTOM AND SIDES OF 10X15X1-INCH JELLYROLL PAN. LINE WITH WAXED PAPER. GREASE AGAIN THOROUGHLY. BREAK EGGS INTO BOWL; ADD SALT, BEAT UNTIL THICK AND LEMON-COLORED. COMBINE SUGAR AND COCOA. ADD GRADUALLY TO EGGS, BEATING WELL AFTER EACH ADDITION. STIR IN VANILLA AND PANCAKE MIX. BEAT UNTIL SMOOTH. SPREAD EVENLY IN PAN. BAKE AT 400°F FOR 12 MINUTES. SPRINKLE A TOWEL GENEROUSLY WITH CONFECTIONERS' SUGAR. LOOSEN EDGES OF CAKE AND TURN OUT ON TOWEL. PEEL OFF WAXED PAPER AND ROLL CAKE UP IN TOWEL. LET STAND 20 MINUTES. MEANWHILE, WHIP CREAM WITH FINE SUGAR. UNROLL CAKE. SPREAD THINLY WITH SOME OF MOCHA-BUTTER CREAM, THEN WITH WHIPPED CREAM. ROLL UP, WRAP FIRMLY IN ALUMINUM FOIL AND CHILL. FROST WITH REMAINING MOCHA-BUTTER CREAM. MARK WITH TIP OF KNIFE OR SMALL SPATULA TO RESEMBLE BARK. CUT OFF A THIN SLICE. UNROLL SLICE, CUT IN HALF, AND REROLL HALVES TO MAKE TWO SMALL "STUMPS." PLACE ON TOP OF ROLL. DECORATE WITH VINE AND LEAVES MADE WITH GREEN ICING. SPRINKLE HERE AND THERE WITH FLAKED COCONUT TO RESEMBLE SNOW. MAKES 12 SERVINGS.

WINTER

"IN THE WINTER, SOMEONE MIGHT HEAR THE DAWN SOUND OF A CARDINAL HURLING ITSELF AGAINST ITS REFLECTION IN A BEDROOM WINDOWPANE, AND THOUGH ASLEEP, SHE MAKES SENSE ENOUGH OF THAT SOUND TO UNDERSTAND WHAT IT IS, SHAKE HER HEAD IN DESPAIR, GET OUT OF BED, GO TO HER STUDY, AND DRAW THE OUTLINE OF AN OWL OR SOME OTHER PREDATOR ON A PIECE OF PAPER, THEN TAPE IT UP ON THE WINDOW BEFORE GOING TO THE KITCHEN AND BREWING A POT OF FRAGRANT, SLIGHTLY ACRID COFFEE.

A NATURAL HISTORY OF THE SENSES   DIANE ACKERMAN, 1990

MOCHA-BUTTER CREAM FROSTING

3/4 POUND UNSALTED BUTTER

3/4 CUP SUGAR

1 1/2 TABLESPOONS UNSWEETENED COCOA

1 1/2 TABLESPOONS INSTANT COFFEE

CREAM BUTTER TO SOFT CONSISTENCY.
COMBINE SUGAR, COCOA, AND INSTANT COFFEE.
SIFT THROUGH FINE SIEVE. ADD
TABLESPOON AT A TIME TO BUTTER,
CONTINUING TO CREAM.

EANS

"O, BOILING, BUBBLING, BERRY, BEAN!
THOU CONSORT OF THE KITCHEN QUEEN—
BROWNED AND GROUND OF EVERY FEATURE,
THE ONLY AROMATIC CREATURE,
FOR WHICH WE LONG, FOR WHICH WE FEEL,
THE BREATH OF MORN, THE PERFUMED MEAL."

OVER THE BLACK COFFEE   ARTHUR GRAY, 1902

THE OURMET'S GUIDE *Selecting The Best*

IN SOME PARTS OF THE WORLD BUYING COFFEE STILL MEANS BUYING GREEN BEANS TO ROAST IN BATCHES AT HOME. HOUSEHOLDS CEREMONIOUSLY GRIND THE ROASTED BEANS BY HAND, ULTIMATELY PREPARING THE DECOCTION ONLY IN PORTIONS LARGE ENOUGH FOR IMMEDIATE CONSUMPTION.

STALING BEGINS THE MOMENT THE COFFEE BEANS LEAVE THE ROASTING MACHINE. THE CARE WITH WHICH THE COFFEE BEANS ARE HANDLED, STORED, AND IF NECESSARY SHIPPED, WILL ALL BE REVEALED IN THE FINAL CUP OF COFFEE.

*C*OFFEE NAMES REFER TO THE BEAN'S PLACE OF ORIGIN, THE STYLE IN WHICH IT IS ROASTED, A PURVEYOR'S PARTICULAR BLEND, OR A FLAVORING ADDED AFTER ROASTING. COFFEE, LIKE WINE, CAN BE LABELED "ESTATE GROWN" OR "VARIETAL."

*F*amiliar *V*arieties:

PACIFIC	NEW GUINEA	GOOD BODY, MODERATE ACIDITY, BROAD FLAVOR
	JAVA	RICH, SMOOTH, FULL-BODIED
	SUMATRA	SWEET, EARTHY, PRONOUNCED HERBAL NUANCES
	SULAWESI	RARE COFFEE, AROMATIC, NUTTY, HERBAL, WOODY
AMERICAS	MEXICO	LIGHT BODY, FRAGRANT AROMA, UNASSERTIVE
	GUATEMALA	LIVELY, ACIDIC, OVERTONES OF SPICE AND CHOCOLATE
	COSTA RICA	FULL-BODIED, DEEP, PUNGENT, HINT OF SMOKINESS
	PANAMA	MEDIUM BODY, FULL FLAVOR, LIVELY
	COLOMBIA	SWEET, ROUNDED FLAVOR, GOOD AFTERTASTE
	KONA	LIGHT, MELLOW, DELICATE, EVANESCENT
AFRICA AND ASIA	KENYA	WELL-BALANCED, SUBLIME, OVERTONES OF BERRIES
	ZIMBABWE	MEDIUM BODY AND ACIDITY, HINT OF LEMON
	TANZANIA	SPICY AROMA, PLEASANT, BALANCED ACIDITY
	ETHIOPIAN FANCY	TANGY, PUNGENT, FLORAL AROMA, FULL FLAVOR
	ARABIAN MOCHA SANANI	PUNGENT, WINY FLAVOR, COMPLEX AROMA
	INDIAN MYSORE	SWEET, SPICY, FULL BODY, MILD, SATISFYING

"MORNING WAS INCOMPLETE WITHOUT THAT CUP OF WELL-BOILED COFFEE WITH CREAM FROM OVERNIGHT MILK....THE FROTH ON THE COFFEE WAS QUICKLY CHASED AROUND THE CUP WITH THE SPOON AND SPOONED INTO THE MOUTH BEFORE IT VANISHED. IT WAS SAID THAT THIS FROTH SIGNIFIED UNEXPECTED MONEY COMING TO THE ONE WHO DRANK THE COFFEE."

THE TASTE OF COUNTRY COOKING   EDNA LEWIS, 1976

BUMPS & GRINDS

While connoisseurs may insist on roasting their own beans, other devotees should rest secure. The best specialty coffee shops roast their own coffee beans or have them roasted by roast masters whose skill and artistry have evolved over long years of training.

LIGHT BROWN; DRY SURFACE	CINNAMON NEW ENGLAND LIGHT	TASTES MORE LIKE TOASTED GRAIN THAN COFFEE, WITH DISTINCT SOUR OR ACIDIC TONES.
MEDIUM BROWN; DRY SURFACE	REGULAR AMERICAN MEDIUM-HIGH BROWN	FOR AN AMERICAN, THE TYPICAL COFFEE FLAVOR; THE GRAIN FLAVOR IS GONE. A DEFINITE ACIDITY SNAP BUT RICHER TONED AND SWEETER THAN LIGHT BROWN.
SLIGHTLY DARKER BROWN; PATCHES OF OIL ON THE SURFACE	LIGHT FRENCH VIENNESE LIGHT ESPRESSO	A SLIGHT, DARK-ROASTED, ALMOST INDISTINGUISHABLE BITTERSWEET TANG. VIENNESE REFERS TO A BLEND OF ONE-THIRD DARK-ROASTED BEANS AND TWO-THIRDS MEDIUM-ROASTED BEANS.
DARK BROWN; OILY SURFACE	ITALIAN ESPRESSO EUROPEAN FRENCH AFTER-DINNER DARK	A DEFINITE BITTERSWEET TANG; ALL ACIDY TONES GONE. EUROPEAN REFERS TO A BLEND OF TWO-THIRDS DARK-ROASTED AND ONE-THIRD MEDIUM-ROASTED BEANS.
VERY DARK BROWN, ALMOST BLACK; VERY SHINY, OILY SURFACE	FRENCH ITALIAN HEAVY SPANISH	BURNED OR CHARCOAL TONES PLUS THE BITTERSWEET TANG; ALL ACIDY TONES ARE GONE.

"COFFEE WAS A FOOD IN THAT HOUSE, NOT A DRINK." A ROMANTIC EDUCATION
PATRICIA HAMPL, 1981

MOST FULL-BODIED COFFEES, WHEN CORRECTLY BREWED, CARRY THEIR FLAVOR THROUGH MILK, WHILE SUGAR IMPARTS ADDITIONAL NUANCES—NOT SIMPLY SWEETNESS. LIQUEURS IN WARM SWEET DRINKS ARE NOT AN INDICATION OF MORAL WEAKNESS.

ESPRESSO
BEST MADE FROM FRENCH OR ITALIAN DARK-ROASTED COFFEE BEANS, FINELY GROUND.

SOLO A SINGLE SHOT, APPROXIMATELY 1½ OUNCES.
DOPPIO TWO FULL SHOTS, APPROXIMATELY 3 OUNCES.
RISTRETTO LESS THAN 1 OUNCE. AN INTENSE CUP.
CON PANNA A SOLO TOPPED WITH WHIPPED CREAM.
ROMANO A SOLO SERVED WITH A TWIST OF LEMON.

CAPPUCCINO
AN EQUAL COMBINATION OF ⅓ ESPRESSO, ⅓ STEAMED MILK, AND ⅓ FROTHED MILK.
CLASSIC A SHOT OF ESPRESSO WITH ONLY FROTHED MILK.

CAFFE LATTE
ESPRESSO WITH STEAMED MILK AND LITTLE OR NO FOAM.

ICED LATTE
1 OR 2 SHOTS OF ESPRESSO WITH A GLASS FULL OF MILK AND ICE.

CAFE CON LECHE
1 SHOT OF ESPRESSO, BOILED MILK, AND SUGAR.

CAFÉ CRÈME
1 ESPRESSO OR FILTERED COFFEE WITH AN EQUAL AMOUNT OF MILK.

FORTIFIED DRINKS
ADD TO A CUP OF ESPRESSO OR FILTERED COFFEE A SHOT OF RUM, WHISKEY, ANISETTE, BRANDY, KAHLUA, TAWNY PORT, OR FRANGELICO.

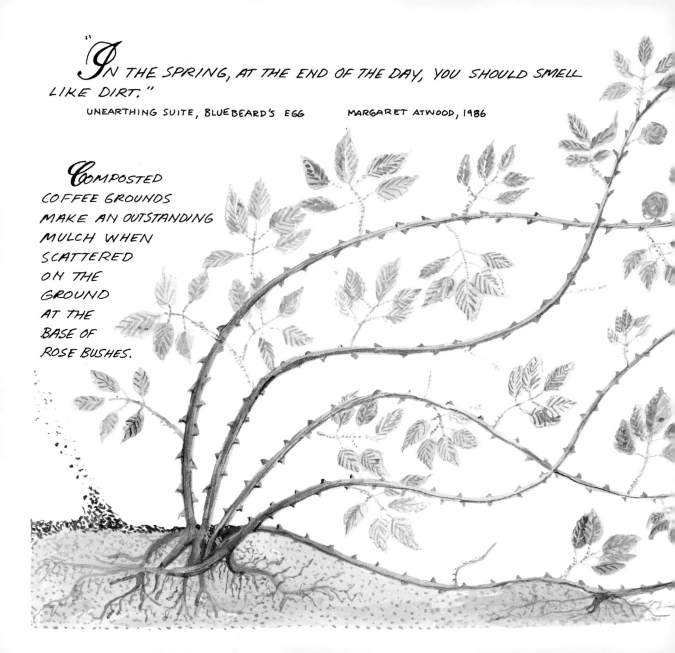

"IN THE SPRING, AT THE END OF THE DAY, YOU SHOULD SMELL LIKE DIRT."

UNEARTHING SUITE, BLUEBEARD'S EGG   MARGARET ATWOOD, 1986

COMPOSTED COFFEE GROUNDS MAKE AN OUTSTANDING MULCH WHEN SCATTERED ON THE GROUND AT THE BASE OF ROSE BUSHES.

REWING the BEST

"*THE COFFEE WAS SO STRONG IT SNARLED AS IT LURCHED OUT OF THE POT.*"

THE EGG AND I   BETTY MACDONALD, 1945

One   START WITH FRESH, COLD WATER. BOTTLED WATER IS PREFERRED FOR ITS NEUTRAL FLAVOR. THE IDEAL TEMPERATURE FOR BREWING IS JUST BELOW BOILING, AROUND 200 DEGREES F. IF THE WATER IS TOO COOL, THE FLAVOR WON'T BE EXTRACTED; IF TOO HOT, THE RESULT IS BITTER COFFEE.

Two   USE THE CORRECT GRIND FOR THE BREWING METHOD CHOSEN. TOO FINE A GRIND WILL PRODUCE BITTER COFFEE; TOO COARSE, WATERY COFFEE. FOR EXAMPLE, OLD-FASHIONED DRIP COFFEE POTS REQUIRE COARSE GRINDS; ESPRESSO COFFEE MAKERS, A FINE GRIND.

Three   MEASURE CAREFULLY, TWO LEVEL TABLESPOONS TO SIX OUNCES OF WATER.

Four AVOID OVER EXTRACTION BY CONTROLLING THE LENGTH OF TIME THE COFFEE IS EXPOSED TO THE WATER. THIS WILL VARY ACCORDING TO THE BREWING SYSTEM OF CHOICE. TOO LONG = BITTER, TOO SHORT = DISHWATER.

Five IF POSSIBLE, USE POTS THAT DON'T REQUIRE PAPER FILTERS, SUCH AS PLUNGER POTS OR ESPRESSO MAKERS. FOR FILTER-TYPE BREWING, USE A GOLD FILTER OR WASH PAPER FILTERS BEFORE USE. BETTER YET, BUY UNBLEACHED PAPER FILTERS.

Six BREW ONLY AS MUCH AS YOU PLAN TO DRINK.

Espresso LOVERS BE AWARE:
THE SIGN OF A WELL-MADE CUP OF ESPRESSO IS THE FROTH OR FOAM ON THE TOP, CALLED THE "CRUST" OR THE "CREMA," WHICH CONTAINS THE CONCENTRATED ESSENCE OF BOTH THE FLAVOR AND THE AROMA.

Pneumatic Filter

E. Cruscan Biggin

German Drip Pot

English French Style Boiler

Filterer

American Coffee Biggin

UNIVERSAL 0012 COFFEE MILL

Coffee Mill

French Drip Pot

Vacuum Machine

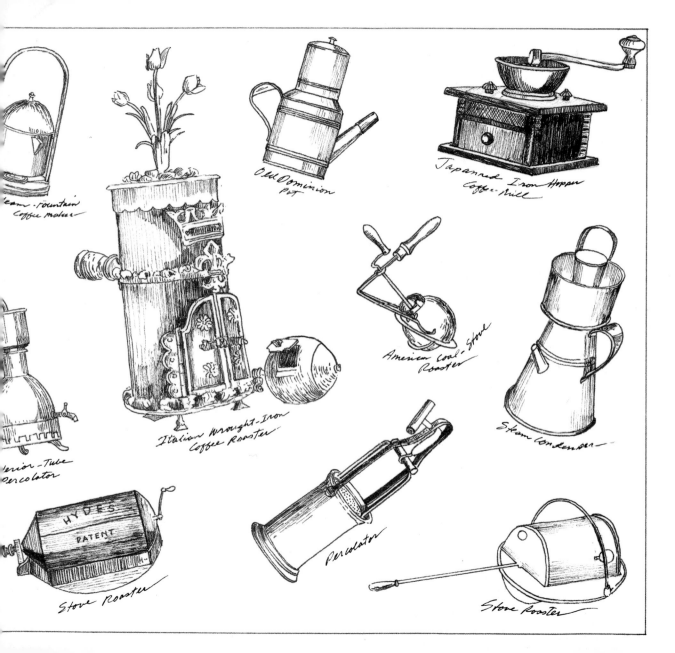

Steam-Fountain
Coffee Maker

Old Dominion
Pot

Japanned Iron Hopper
Coffee Mill

American Coal-Stove
Roaster

Interior-Tube
Percolator

Italian Wrought-Iron
Coffee Roaster

Steam Condenser

HYDES.
PATENT

Stove Roaster

Percolator

Stove Roaster

AROMA

"JELLIES PRETTIFIED WITH DYES, ARMOUR-PLATED CAKES AND PIES
WHICH WOULD KNOCK A BUZZARD FLAT WITHOUT WARNING
I CAN MERRILY DIGEST WITH A GUSTATORY ZEST
IF MY COFFEE'S ONLY DECENT IN THE MORNING.
--- I WANDER IN A COMA IF I MISS THAT FRESH AROMA
OF A FRAGRANT CUP OF COFFEE IN THE MORNING!"

GROUNDS FOR COMPLAINT   BERTON BRALEY, 1935

The Tasters' Glossary

MODERN CULTIVATION, PROCESSING, AND SHIPPING HAVE TRANSFORMED THE ONCE ELITE AND EXOTIC ELIXIR INTO AN ACCESSIBLE LUXURY. FINE COFFEE OFFERS ALL THE VARIETY, COMPLEXITY, AND SUBTLETY OF FINE WINE.

A "CUPPER," OR PROFESSIONAL TASTER, METICULOUSLY EXAMINES COFFEE, STARTING WITH THE "CHOPS," OR RAW BEAN SAMPLES. THE METHODICALLY BREWED BEVERAGE IS SLURPED OFF A SPOON, SWISHED IN THE MOUTH, AND SPIT INTO A SPITTOON. KITCHEN CONNOISSEURS CAN INVENT A MORE PERSONAL RITUAL FOR SNIFFING, SIPPING, SAMPLING, AND CONSIDERING SOME OF COFFEE'S UNIQUE CHARACTERISTICS.

ACIDITY — SHARP, PIQUANT, PLEASANT QUALITY THAT IMPARTS SNAP, LIVELINESS, OR VERVE.

AROMA — PERFUME OR ODOR: LACKING, FAINT, MODERATE, STRONG OR FRAGRANT.

BAKED — UNDERDEVELOPED, EITHER FROM BEING ROASTED TOO LONG OR AT TOO LOW A TEMPERATURE.

BITTER — HARSH FLAVOR DETECTED ON THE BACK OF THE TONGUE DUE TO OVER-ROASTING OR OVER-EXTRACTION.

BODY — IMPRESSION OF WEIGHT AND TEXTURE: WATERY, THIN, SLIGHT, LIGHT, BUTTERY, OILY, RICH, SMOOTH, OR CHEWY.

CINNAMON — A SPICY NUANCE.

COCOA — A SWEETISH SMELL OF STALE OR FADED ROASTED COFFEE AFTER EXPOSURE TO AIR.

Dirty — UNCLEAN SMELL AND TASTE; MIGHT IMPLY EARTHINESS, MUSTINESS, OR SOURNESS.

Flavor — THE OVERALL IMPRESSION, COMBINING AROMA, ACIDITY, AND BODY.

Fruity — TAINTED FLAVOR FROM OVERRIPE FRUIT PULP.

Grassy — TAINTED FLAVOR DUE TO SWAMP-WATER WASHING OR IMPROPER DRYING.

Green — FLAVOR OF COFFEE HARVESTED TOO EARLY.

Hard OR **Harsh** — OPPOSITE OF SWEET OR MILD.

Hidy — SMELL OF LEATHER FROM IMPROPER STORAGE.

Mellow — WELL-BALANCED OR SOFT FLAVOR.

Nutty — COFFEE THAT LACKS COFFEE FLAVOR.

Past-Croppish — COFFEE THAT HAS DETERIORATED PRIOR TO ROASTING SO THAT IT TASTES STRAW- OR HAY-LIKE.

Rio-y — MEDICINAL IODINE FLAVOR TYPICAL OF POOREST GRADE BRAZILIAN COFFEE.

Rubbery — HAVING THE ODOR OF BURNT RUBBER.

Strong — DESCRIBES THE INTENSITY OF DEFECTS OR VIRTUES IN FLAVOR.

Wild — EXTREME FLAVOR NUANCES.

Winy — MELLOW, THICK BODY - QUALITY OF CERTAIN FINE COFFEE.

A Plain Cup of Joe at Eight

5:00 A.M., Barcelona: CAFE CON LECHE AND BUÑUELOS PASTRIES ARE CONSUMED BY THE YOUNG AND THE YOUNG AT HEART AFTER YET ANOTHER NIGHT ON THE TOWN.

6:00 A.M., El Paso: HERD BEHAVIOR PREVAILS ON A STAMPEDE OF DESPERADOES UNTIL THEIR COWBOY COFFEE OF COARSE GROUNDS AND STREAM WATER IS BOILED TO A FINE METALLIC BREW AND SERVED PIPING HOT FROM ITS TIN CAMPFIRE KETTLE.

10:30 A.M., Cincinnati, AMONG OTHERS: ACCORDING TO UNIVERSAL HABIT, PHYSIOLOGICAL NEED, AND MEDIOCRE TASTES, A SLUG IN THE MUG OF INSTANT DISHWATER COFFEE IS CONSUMED BY FACTORY WORKERS, FARMHANDS, COMPUTER PROGRAMMERS, ACE SECRETARIES, THEIR BOSSES, AND SEVERAL MILLION OTHERS DURING THIS COFFEE BREAK.

our Coffee From Here to There

2:00 P.M., Istanbul: NO TIME TO LOSE FACE BY "LOSING THE FACE" OR THE FOAM OF TURKISH COFFEE. THREE OUNCES OF WATER IS BOILED TOGETHER WITH ONE TEASPOON OF PULVERIZED DARK ROASTED COFFEE AND THE SAME AMOUNT OF SUGAR. (FOR WEDDINGS, MORE SUGAR IS ADDED. FOR FUNERALS, IT'S NEVER SWEETENED.) ONE HALF OF THIS DECOCTION IS POURED INTO TALL CYLINDRICAL CUPS, THE REST IS BOILED AGAIN AND POURED WITH TREMBLING HANDS ON TOP TO ACHIEVE THIS INFAMOUS MOUSSE-LIKE BEVERAGE.

4:00 P.M., San Francisco: THE SOUND OF FOAMING MILK STEAMERS IS HEARD EMANATING FROM ANY OF THE DOZENS OF "ESPRESSO TO GO" BARS SERVING CAFFE LATTES FOR "TEATIME."

10:30 P.M., Paris: A DECADENT FIVE-COURSE SUPPER IS FOLLOWED BY A DEMITASSE OF THE DIVINE DIGESTIVE.

1:00 A.M., New York City: UP NUMBER FIVE AND COUNTING, THIS AUTOMATIC DINER DRIP, PRONOUNCED "CAWF-FEE," FUELS UNDISCOVERED AUTHOR'S STRUGGLE TO CREATE THE NEXT GREAT AMERICAN NOVEL.

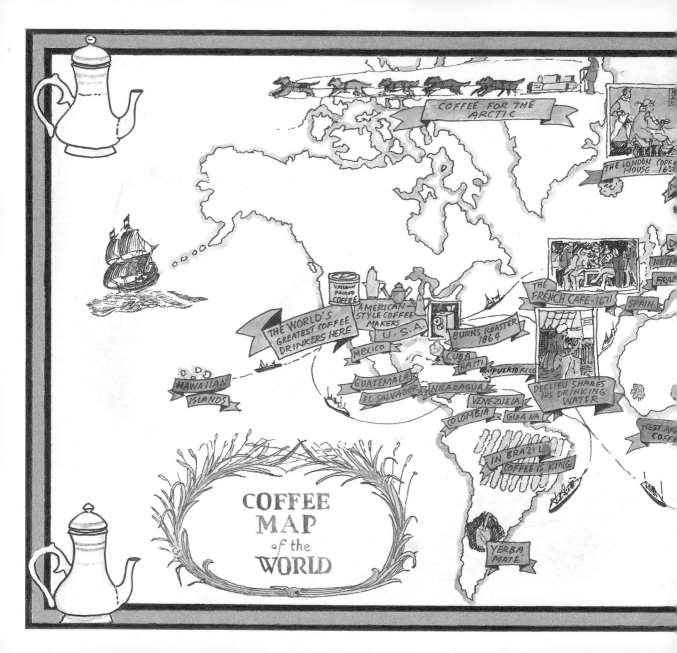

COFFEE FOR THE ARCTIC

THE LONDON COFFEE HOUSE 1637

THE WORLD'S GREATEST COFFEE DRINKERS HERE

AMERICAN-STYLE COFFEE MAKERS U.S.A.

VACUUM PACKED COFFEE

THE FRENCH CAFÉ - 1671

NETH...

FRAN...

SPAIN

BURNS ROASTER 1864

MEXICO

CUBA

HAITI

PUERTO RICO

GUATEMALA

EL SALVADOR

NICARAGUA

VENEZUELA

DECLIEU SHARES HIS DRINKING WATER

HAWAIIAN ISLANDS

COLOMBIA

GUIANA

WEST AFRICA COFFEE

IN BRAZIL COFFEE IS KING

COFFEE MAP of the WORLD

YERBA MATE

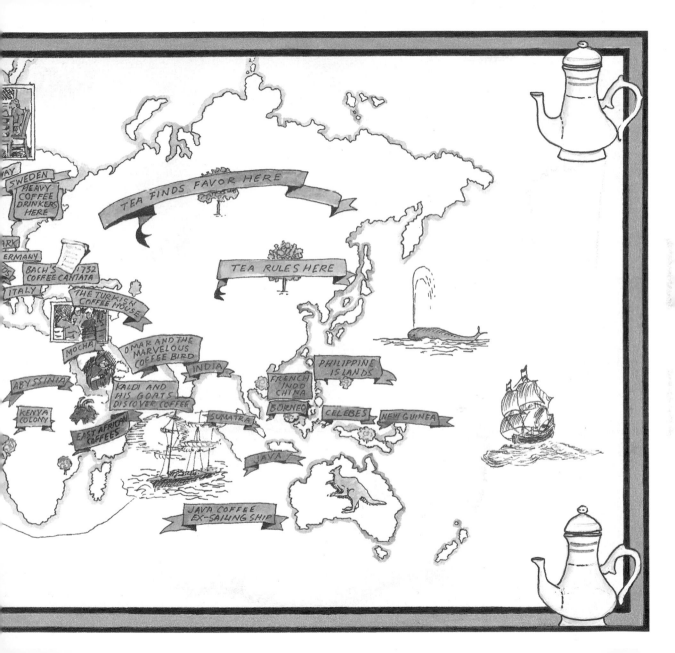

SUMMER

In Portofino they're called crostatine di frutta fresca; in London, they're fresh fruit tartlets. Made by busy little bees on summer break they're dessert "nests" rolled and squished and shaped and reshaped from pastry crust then filled with whipped cream or vanilla custard and topped with sliced strawberries, raspberries, blackberries, pears, apricots, peaches — handpicked, preferably. Serve with "children's coffee" made from a teaspoon of molasses and cold milk. Add two straws. For grown-ups try this recipe for island coffee.

ISLAND COFFEE

This chilled espresso with a kick makes a delightful end to a Caribbean meal.

1 teaspoon superfine sugar
½ cup espresso coffee
2 tablespoons Myer's rum or other dark, heavy rum
1 tablespoon Tia Maria liquor
2 tablespoons heavy cream

Dissolve the sugar in the espresso and chill.

Pour the rum and Tia Maria into an 8-ounce stemmed glass and add the espresso mixture. Slowly pour the cream over the back of a teaspoon so the cream floats on top.

Serves 1

Summer Iced Fruitcake

1½ CUPS SIFTED FLOUR
½ TEASPOON SALT
½ TEASPOON BAKING SODA
½ TEASPOON CLOVES
½ TEASPOON NUTMEG
½ TEASPOON CINNAMON
1 CUP CHOPPED, MIXED
   CANDIED FRUIT

½ CUP CHOPPED WALNUTS
½ CUP BUTTER OR MARGARINE
½ CUP BROWN SUGAR,
   FIRMLY PACKED
2 EGGS
½ CUP MOLASSES
1 TEASPOON LEMON EXTRACT
COFFEE ICING (RECIPE FOLLOWS)

COMBINE THE FLOUR, SALT, SODA AND SPICES. DREDGE FRUIT AND NUTS WITH 1 TABLESPOON FLOUR MIXTURE. IN A SEPARATE BOWL, CREAM THE BUTTER WITH THE SUGAR. ADD EGGS, MIXING UNTIL LIGHT AND FLUFFY. ADD MOLASSES; BLEND WELL. ADD FRUIT, NUTS AND EXTRACT ALONG WITH THE FLOUR MIXTURE; MIX WELL. POUR INTO A GREASED, WAXED-PAPER-LINED 9x5-INCH LOAF PAN. BAKE AT 300°F FOR 1 HOUR 45 MINUTES. WHILE THE FRUIT CAKE IS COOLING, MAKE ICING.

Coffee Icing

2 TABLESPOONS BUTTER OR MARGARINE
1½ CUPS SIFTED CONFECTIONERS'
   SUGAR

1½ TEASPOONS LIGHT CREAM
2 TEASPOONS INSTANT COFFEE
¼ CUP CHOPPED WALNUTS

CREAM BUTTER OR MARGARINE UNTIL LIGHT AND FLUFFY. GRADUALLY ADD SUGAR; BEAT UNTIL SMOOTH. ADD CREAM AND COFFEE; BEAT WELL. SPREAD ON TOP OF FRUITCAKE, SPRINKLE WITH CHOPPED NUTS.

Linzertorte

1 cup butter or margarine
1 cup sugar
1 tablespoon grated orange or lemon peel
2 egg yolks
1½ cups flour, sifted
1 teaspoon baking powder
2 teaspoons cinnamon

½ teaspoon cloves
¼ teaspoon salt
1 cup ground nuts (filberts, almonds, or walnuts)
1 cup plum preserves

Whipped cream

Cream the butter; add sugar slowly while continuing to cream. Add orange or lemon peel. Add egg yolks one at a time, beating well after each addition. Mix and sift flour, baking powder, spices, and salt. Add slowly, stirring in. Stir in the nuts. After all is added, mix by hand until all ingredients are thoroughly combined. Chill. Pat two-thirds of dough into bottom of a 9-inch layer-cake pan (preferably one with removable bottom). Spread preserves over this layer. Roll out remaining dough; cut into 8 strips ¾ inch wide and place lattice fashion on top of preserves. Bake in a 350°F oven for 50 to 60 minutes or until edges of strips recede from sides of pan. Remove from pan. Cool. Garnish with a frill of whipped cream. Cut into small wedges to serve. Makes 10 to 12 servings.

ENGLAND: THE ONE PENNY UNIVERSITY

OWNERS OF ENGLISH TAVERNS AND ALE HOUSES MALIGNED COFFEE HOPING TO WIN BACK CUSTOMERS. THEY DERIDED IT AS "TURKEY-GRUEL, NINNY BROTH, ESSENCE OF OLD SHOES, SYRROP OF SOOT, A LOATHSOME POTION, NOT YET UNDERSTOOD."

ALL ABOUT COFFEE   WILLIAM UKERS, 1935

THROUGHOUT ENGLAND, THE COFFEEHOUSE WAS CALLED THE ONE PENNY UNIVERSITY. FOR THAT PRICE ALL COULD ENTER THE CAFE, IMBIBE, AND EDUCATE THEMSELVES BY LISTENING TO THE DISCUSSIONS AND READING THE NEWSPAPERS AVAILABLE.

KING GEORGE II SAID THEY WERE SEMINARIES OF SEDITION.

IN LONDON, FOR INSTANCE, EACH COFFEEHOUSE HAD ITS OWN PARTICULAR CLIENTELE. SURGEONS AND PATIENTS MET AT BASTON'S, BOOKSELLERS AND PLAYWRIGHTS AT THE BALTIC.

COFFEE HOUSE JESTS

EDWARD LLOYD'S COFFEEHOUSE WAS A MEETING PLACE FOR SEAFARERS AND MERCHANTS. LLOYD LOVED TO MAKE LISTS, SO FOR THE CONVENIENCE OF HIS CUSTOMERS HE KEPT LOGS OF WHAT SHIPS WERE CARRYING WHAT FOR WHOM AND WHICH SHIPS NEEDED INSURANCE FOR WHAT. THE INFORMAL OPERATION EVOLVED INTO THE LLOYD'S OF LONDON COMPANY. TODAY LLOYD'S OF LONDON'S UNIFORMED ATTENDANTS IN THEIR INSURANCE OFFICES ARE STILL REFERRED TO AS WAITERS.

Dunking Recipes: More Than Doughnuts

The popular term "dunk," which describes the practice of dipping something tasty to eat into coffee, came to the United States from Europe. During World War II, American servicemen relaxing in European cafes learned that what they were doing with their pastry and coffee was called "junking." Back home, the cockney-yiddish word merged with the pennsylvania german word "dunken" to yield the colloquial dunk.

Doughnuts

1 pound vegetable shortening
2 2/3 cups sifted flour
4 teaspoons double-acting baking powder
1 teaspoon salt
1/2 cup sugar
1/4 teaspoon nutmeg
1/2 teaspoon cinnamon
2 eggs, well beaten
1/2 cup milk
1 teaspoon vanilla
3 tablespoons melted shortening

Heat the vegetable shortening to 365°F (to test, a cube of bread dropped in the oil should brown in 60 seconds). Sift together dry ingredients. Combine eggs, milk, and vanilla. Add liquid to dry ingredients. Mix just enough to moisten dry ingredients thoroughly. Add melted shortening. Roll out 1/4 inch thick on a floured board. Cut with a doughnut cutter, and fry in hot shortening. Do not fry more than 3 or 4 at a time or the fat will cool too rapidly. Fry 3 to 5 minutes or until delicately brown, turning once. Drain well. Place on absorbent paper. Makes 20 doughnuts (using a 2 1/2-inch cutter.)

Soda Bread

2 CUPS ALL-PURPOSE FLOUR
3/4 TEASPOON BAKING SODA
1/2 TEASPOON SALT
1 TABLESPOON SUGAR
6 TABLESPOONS SHORTENING

1/2 CUP LIGHT, SEEDLESS RAISINS
1 TABLESPOON CARAWAY SEEDS
1/4 CUP VINEGAR
1/2 CUP MILK

MIX AND SIFT FLOUR, BAKING SODA, SALT, AND SUGAR. CUT IN SHORTENING WITH TWO KNIVES OR PASTRY BLENDER. STIR IN RAISINS AND CARAWAY SEEDS. COMBINE VINEGAR AND MILK. ADD TO FLOUR MIXTURE AND BLEND WITH A FORK. TURN INTO GREASED 8-INCH, LAYER-CAKE PAN 1 1/2 INCHES DEEP; PAT SMOOTH. BAKE IN A 375°F OVEN, 30 MINUTES OR UNTIL DONE.   MAKES ONE LOAF

Individual Coffee Cakes

1/4 CUP SHORTENING
1 1/3 CUPS SUGAR, DIVIDED
2 EGG YOLKS
1 1/4 CUPS FLOUR, SIFTED
2 TEASPOONS BAKING POWDER

1/2 TEASPOON SALT
1/2 CUP MILK
2 EGG WHITES
1/2 TEASPOON CINNAMON
1/2 CUP CHOPPED WALNUTS

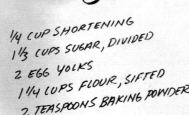

CREAM THE SHORTENING. ADD 1 CUP OF THE SUGAR GRADUALLY AND CREAM THOROUGHLY. BEAT EGG YOLKS. ADD TO THE CREAMED MIXTURE. MIX AND SIFT FLOUR, BAKING POWDER, AND SALT; ADD ALTERNATELY WITH MILK. BEAT EGG WHITES UNTIL STIFF BUT NOT DRY. FOLD IN. POUR INTO WELL-GREASED MUFFIN TINS. MIX 1/3 CUP SUGAR WITH CINNAMON AND CHOPPED WALNUTS. SPRINKLE OVER THE BATTER. BAKE IN A 375°F OVEN, 20 TO 25 MINUTES.

SERVE HOT.   SERVES 8.

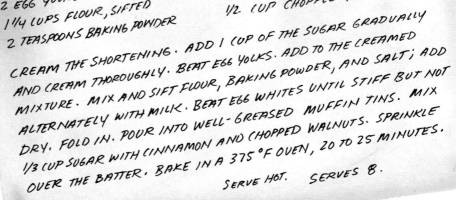
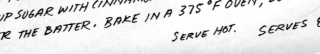

AMERICA: THE COFFEE REVOLUTION

"...WHEREVER IT HAS BEEN INTRODUCED IT HAS SPELLED REVOLUTION. IT HAS BEEN THE WORLD'S MOST RADICAL DRINK IN THAT ITS FUNCTION HAS ALWAYS BEEN TO MAKE PEOPLE THINK. AND WHEN PEOPLE BEGIN TO THINK, THEY BECOME DANGEROUS TO TYRANTS AND FOES OF LIBERTY OF THOUGHTS AND ACTIONS."

ALL ABOUT COFFEE   WILLIAM UKERS, 1935

BOSTON'S GREEN DRAGON COFFEE HOUSE DOMINATED UNION STREET FOR 135 YEARS, BEGINNING IN 1697, AND BECAME KNOWN AS THE HEADQUARTERS OF THE AMERICAN REVOLUTION.

IN NEW YORK IN 1791, THE TONTINE COFFEEHOUSE, ONE OF THE MOST PRETENTIOUSLY DECORATED BUILDINGS IN THE CITY, DOUBLED AS THE STOCK EXCHANGE.

"THE BIG COFFEE POT"

ONE OF THE CITY'S OLD LANDMARKS, WINSTON-SALEM, N. C.

According to the French statesman Talleyrand (1754-1838): New Orleans Creoles claimed they preferred to drink their indispensable coffee "noir comme le diable, chaud comme l'enfer, pur comme un ange, doux comme l'amour." Black as the devil, hot as hell, pure as an angel, sweet as love.

American settlers, scouts, shepherds, soldiers, and cowboys liked their coffee hot, black, and strong enough to walk by itself.

Take five, folks:

Before the industrial revolution, the duties and pleasures of life flowed together in a seamless coffee continuum.

When the urge overcame a weary farmer in the countryside or a cobbler in the city, the laborers would lay down their tools and wander into their kitchens to revitalize themselves with a bracing cup of coffee. Over the brew, they rekindled their energy and chatted with other family members before resuming their daily tasks.

The advent of factory labor marked the demise of the day's traditional ebb and flow. To compensate, employers instituted ...

THE COFFEE BREAK.

"It's Just a Cup of Coffee" to You But a Reputation to Us...

GIDDYAP ! L' DOGGIE!

Cecil Smith

Coffee on The Range

AUTUMN

"FOR FORTY YEARS THIS HAS BEEN THE MAIN EVENT OF THE SEASON.... WE WOULD START THE DAY WITH A GOOD HEARTY BREAKFAST OF GRIDDLE CAKES, SAUSAGES, HOT BREAD, PRESERVES, JAM, AND LOTS OF HOT COFFEE TO BRACE US FOR THE BRISK NOVEMBER WEATHER."

THE TASTE OF COUNTRY COOKING
EDNA LEWIS, 1976

Florentine Country Picnic

PANINI AL TARTUFFO : MUSHROOM PÂTÉ
SANDWICHES SERVED WITH SLICED COMICE PEARS,
A THERMOS OF ESPRESSO, AND A SHOT OF GRAPPA.

Mushroom Pâté

SAUTE 1 POUND MUSHROOMS. LET COOL, THEN
MINCE. ADD SALT AND PEPPER TO TASTE. ADD
MASCARPONE (YOU CAN SUBSTITUTE CRÈME
FRAÏCHE, SOUR CREAM OR CREAM CHEESE)
TO TASTE. MIX UNTIL THE CONSISTENCY OF
A PASTE. REFRIGERATE UNTIL READY TO
USE. SPREAD ON CRUSTY BREAD OR CRACKERS.

Italy: Literati e Glitterati

The cultural and political life associated with Italian cafes led to the publication in Milan of a periodical, starting in 1764, entitled "Il Caffe." The review was provocatively different from the other pompous reviews of the period. More than a beverage, coffee seemed to be a catalyst for clarity of thought.

Sit and sip an espresso in the same chair where Casanova, Goethe, Dickens, Proust, and countless other famous people once sat.

Since the 18th century, when Italy's great cafes appeared, the famous from around the world have frequented these living legends from the "Golden Age" which still thrive today:

ROME	CAFFE GRECO
ROME	CAFFE ARAGNO
NAPLES	CAFFE GAMBRINUS
FLORENCE	CAFFE GIUBBE ROSA
FLORENCE	CAFFE GILLI
VENICE	CAFFE FLORIAN
VENICE	CAFFE QUADRI
PADUA	CAFFE PEDROCCHI
TRIESTE	CAFFE SAN MARCO
TURIN	CAFFE PLATTI

CAFFE GIUBBE ROSA
CAFFE QUADRI
CAFFE FLORIAN
CAFFE ARAGNO
CAFFE PLATTI
CAFFE GAMBRINUS
CAFFE SAN MARCO
CAFFE GILLI

France: Cafe Society

The French writer Voltaire, one of the leaders of the Age of Reason, is said to have drunk fifty cups of coffee a day. Historian Jules Michelet described 18th-century Paris as a coffeehouse drunken on lucidity.

CAFE RESTAURANT

AUBERGE DU CLOU

30, Avenue Trudaine, Paris

Since its inception, the French cafe has always been the ideal place to rendezvous with a lover, to accuse a spouse, to create a literary masterpiece, to study the latest hemunes, or to denounce a government; the Bastille fell two days after an impassioned speech was made atop a table at the Cafe Foy.

Start the day with a croissant or pain-beurre, a chunk of baguette with butter, and a cafe creme, the French version of a cappuccino. Or savor cafe au lait at home in a large ceramic bowl that warms the hands and soothes the complexion with rising steam. Proper preparation of cafe au lait requires pouring equal parts of coffee and warm milk from two different pitchers into the bowl at the same time.

In France, the term "a coffee," or "un cafe," is generally assumed to mean a coffee with hot milk in the morning, but by mid-morning is interpreted as a demitasse or espresso.

I HAVE A PARTICULAR PASSION FOR BOOKSTORE CAFES.
I IMBIBE THAT HEADY THINKERS' TONIC, FEEL REJUVENATED ENOUGH TO
BROWSE, PONDER, AND WANDER FOR LONGER THAN I SHOULD. INEVITABLY,
I PURCHASE SOMETHING WONDERFUL.

*Y*OUR FAVORITE PLACES

I LOVE TO SIT IN CREATION'S CAFE LOOKING OUT FROM A PERCH ON OUR BACK DECK, DRINKING IN MOTHER NATURE BETWEEN FREQUENT SIPS OF MY OWN BEST BREW.

*Y*OUR FAVORITE PLACES

I'VE BEEN KNOWN TO WAIT FOR A FULL MOON TO PLANT BUT NEVER TO DRINK COFFEE, THANK GOODNESS!

*Y*OUR FAVORITE RECIPES FOR SPRING

*S*UMMER IS ABOUT GARDENS AND BUGS AND ETERNALLY LONG DAYS AND ICED GRANITA IN TALL FROSTY GLASSES WITH WHIPPED CREAM AND SHAVED CHOCOLATE!

*Y*OUR FAVORITE RECIPES FOR SUMMER

Someone once suggested I top a barbequed leg of lamb with a hot coffee glaze. I'm not sure?... Sounds like something one would eat for Halloween.

Your favorite recipes for Autumn

Nothing warms the cockles of my heart and the tips of my frozen toes like a cup of steaming mochaccino with a dash of Frangelico.

Your favorite recipes for winter

THANK YOU

My HUMBLE THANKS FOR ALL THE GREAT HELP AND ENCOURAGEMENT I RECEIVED ON THESE BOOKS FROM FAMILY AND FRIENDS AND IN PARTICULAR ...

... THE LOVELY AND TALENTED LADIES OF COLLINS PUBLISHERS SAN FRANCISCO WHO WORKED ESPECIALLY HARD ON THIS BOOK.

JENNIFER BARRY, MAURA CAREY DAMACION, JULIE BERNATZ, DAYNA MACY, KARI PERIN, AND MORE "JENNIFERS" THAN ONE CAN SHAKE A COFFEE SPOON AT, INCLUDING JENNIFER WARD, JENNIFER COLLINS, AND JENNIFER GRACE!

... TO JONATHAN MILLS, ALSO OF COLLINS PUBLISHERS, FOR HIS BRILLIANT ATTENTION TO VERY TRICKY PRODUCTION DETAILS -- ESPECIALLY ON THESE BOOKS.

--- TO SHELLEI ADDISON FOR HER WONDERFUL TEXT CONTRIBUTIONS AND TO ALL OF HER EDITORIAL ARTS CREW AT FLYING FISH BOOKS.

--- TO MY DAUGHTERS SUNNY AND WENDY KOCH FOR THEIR INCREDIBLE ASSISTANCE ON DESIGN AND LAYOUT AND MK GRAPHIC BUSINESS.

--- TO OUR FRIENDS STEVE FLETCHER AND CARL CROFT OF TAMPOPO INC. FOR THEIR WONDERFUL SUPPLY OF COFFEE ACCESSORIES, BOOKS AND INFORMATION.

--- AND TO MY RELENTLESS PARTNER AND DEAR FRIEND, KRISTIN JOYCE, FOR STARING INTO SEVERAL CAFFE LATTES AND SEEING BOOK AFTER BOOK APPEAR BEFORE HER EYES!